POLICE TELEPHONE

FREE

FOR USE OF

PUBLIC

Statistics

DEBUT	*Rose* (2005)
PLAYED BY	Noel Clarke
HOME	London, England
STATUS	Friend
HEIGHT	1.75m
SCARE RATING	Not applicable
SPECIAL FEATURES	Good with computers
WEAPONS	Not applicable
LIKES	Rose Tyler
DISLIKES	Being left behind
TALK	'I'm not the tin dog — and I wanna see what's out there.'

British Library Cataloguing-in-Publication Data:
A catalogue record for this book is available from the British Library

ISBN 1 84425 427 5

Library of Congress catalog card no. 2006938247

Published by Haynes Publishing,
Sparkford, Yeovil, Somerset BA22 7JJ, UK
Tel: 01963 442030 Fax: 01963 440001
Int. tel: +44 1963 442030 Int. fax: +44 1963 440001
Email: sales@haynes.co.uk
Website: www.haynes.co.uk

Haynes North America, Inc.,
861 Lawrence Drive, Newbury Park
California 91320, USA

Printed and bound in Great Britain by
J. H. Haynes & Co. Ltd, Sparkford

The Author

Moray Laing is the Editor of *Doctor Who Adventures* magazine.
He is a life-long follower of all things *Who*.

About

Top Trumps

It's now more than 30 years since Britain's kids first caught the Top Trumps craze. The game remained hugely popular until the 1990s, when it slowly drifted into obscurity. Then, in 1999, UK games company Winning Moves discovered it, bought it, dusted it down, gave it a thorough makeover and introduced it to a whole new generation. And so the Top Trumps legend continues.

Nowadays, there are Top Trumps titles for just about everyone, with subjects about animals, cars, ships, aircraft and all the great films and TV shows. Top Trumps is now even more popular than before. In Britain, a pack of Top Trumps is bought every six seconds! And it's not just British children who love the game. Children in Australasia, the Far East, the Middle East, all over Europe and in North America can buy Top Trumps at their local shops.

Today you can even play the game on the internet, interactive DVD, your games console and even your mobile phone.

You've played the game...

TOP TRUMPS®

DOCTOR · WHO

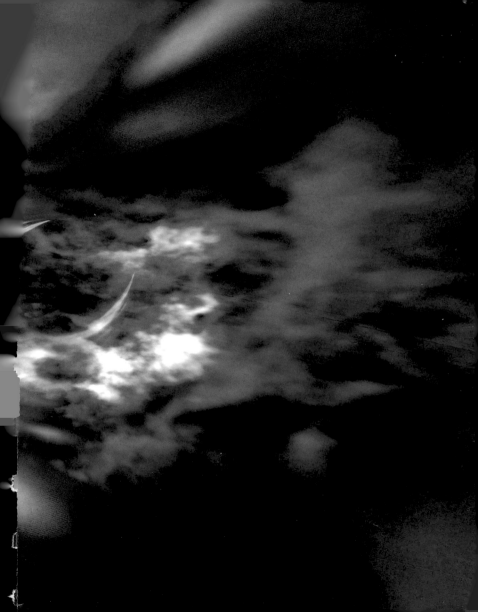

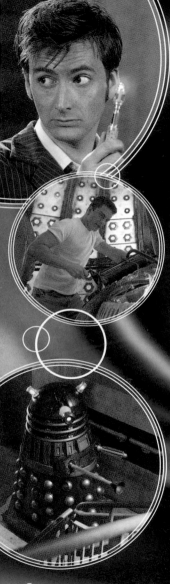

Contents

Rogue Time Agent

Captain Jack Harkness comes from the 51st century – and was a long way from home when the Doctor and Rose first met him. He tried to sell them a crashed spaceship in 1940s London. A former Time Agent, he woke up one morning and found that the agents had stolen memory of two years of his life. The reasons for this are unknown, but it has left Jack very wary about the whole agency. After helping the time travellers prevent a plague of gas-mask zombies take over the world, Jack was rescued by the Doctor and he travelled in the TARDIS for a while. A brave fighter, he played an important role in helping to defeat the Daleks on the Game Station but was exterminated by the evil creatures. Jack was brought back to life by Rose, while she had the power of the vortex running through her, but the TARDIS left the Game Station without him.

Statistics

DEBUT	*The Empty Child* (2005)
PLAYED BY	John Barrowman
HOME	Unknown
STATUS	Friend
HEIGHT	1.85m
SCARE RATING	Not applicable
SPECIAL FEATURES	Has loads of alien tech
WEAPONS	Sonic blaster
LIKES	Flirting
DISLIKES	Cowards
TALK	'I like to think of myself as a criminal.'

Sarah Jane Smith
Journalist and former time traveller

Before Rose travelled in the TARDIS, the Doctor used to know a journalist called Sarah Jane Smith. Like Rose, Sarah Jane enjoyed travelling in time and space. The Doctor was forced to leave Sarah Jane on Earth when he was called back to his home planet in the days when humans weren't allowed there and it was still around. He later built her a robot dog called K-9 and left it with her as a surprise present. Years later the old friends bumped into each other when the Krillitanes took over Deffry Vale School. Sarah Jane knew there was something strange going on at the school, so decided to do a bit of undercover investigating and stumbled upon the TARDIS again. Jealous at first, it took a while for Sarah Jane and Rose to warm to each other, and she admitted how hard she found life without the Doctor.

Statistics

MODERN DEBUT	*School Reunion* (2006)
PLAYED BY	Elisabeth Sladen
HOME	London, England
STATUS	Friend
HEIGHT	1.61m
SCARE RATING	Not applicable
SPECIAL FEATURES	Owns a robot dog called K-9
WEAPONS	Not applicable
LIKES	Finding danger and excitement, the Doctor, investigating
DISLIKES	Injustice, alien threats, Rose Tyler (at first!)
TALK	'You took me to the furthest reaches of the galaxy, you showed me supernovas, intergalactic battles... and then you just dropped me back on Earth.'

K-9
The Doctor's old robot dog

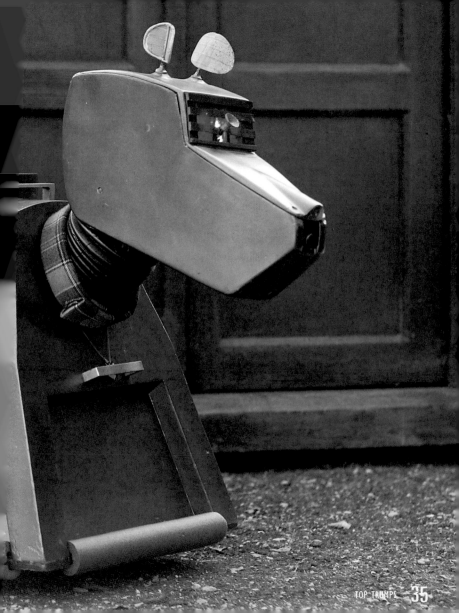

K-9

The Doctor's old robot dog

K-9 is a highly intelligent robot dog. There have been four models of K-9 so far, three of which were built by the Doctor. The Time Lord met the original K-9 in the year 5000AD. A professor had built the robot because he wasn't allowed to take his own pet dog into space with him. This K-9 travelled with the Doctor for a while until the robot decided to stay with the Doctor's friend Leela. The Doctor built a second model, which helped him find the Key to Time. After many adventures he was eventually damaged by dangerous Time Winds and had to leave the TARDIS. A third model was given to Sarah Jane Smith on Earth – a present from the Doctor so the robot could look after his old friend. This model was blown up while fighting the Krillitanes, so the Doctor built a fourth K-9 for Sarah Jane to replace him.

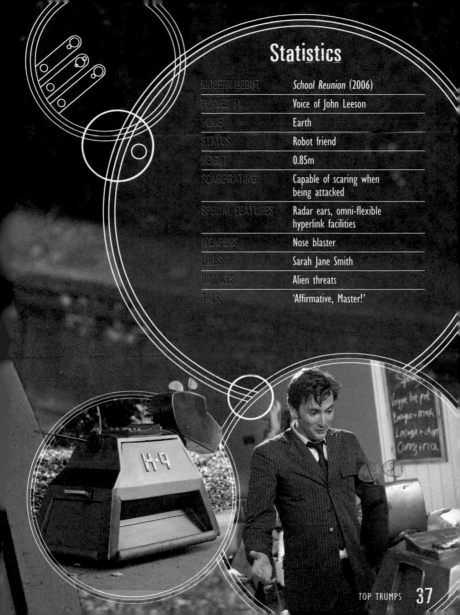

Statistics

MODERN DEBUT	*School Reunion* (2006)
PLAYED BY	Voice of John Leeson
HOME	Earth
STATUS	Robot friend
HEIGHT	0.85m
SCARE RATING	Capable of scaring when being attacked
SPECIAL FEATURES	Radar ears, omni-flexible hyperlink facilities
WEAPONS	Nose blaster
LIKES	Sarah Jane Smith
DISLIKES	Alien threats
TALK	'Affirmative, Master!'

Jackie Tyler

Rose's mum

Jackie Tyler
Rose's mum

Jackie Tyler is Rose's mum and, like Rose, her life changed when the Doctor appeared. When her daughter vanished for a year, Jackie spent twelve months searching for her and blaming Rose's old boyfriend Mickey for her disappearance. Jackie made Mickey's life miserable during that time – but they later became good friends again. When Rose reappeared, Jackie couldn't understand where she had been – and blamed the Doctor for stealing her away. She even slapped him! When she discovered Rose had become an adventurer in time and space, and travelled in the TARDIS, she made the Doctor promise that he would look after her, a promise he always kept. Jackie was always happiest when Rose popped back to see her now and again. She ended up living with a parallel version of her late husband Pete on a parallel Earth with Rose and Mickey.

Statistics

DEBUT	*Rose* (2005)
PLAYED BY	Camille Coduri
HOME	London, England
STATUS	Friend
HEIGHT	1.65m
SCARE RATING	Not applicable unless she's angry
SPECIAL FEATURES	Good at making tea in a crisis
WEAPONS	None, but her scream is powerful
LIKES	Her daughter Rose
DISLIKES	Meeting monsters like the 'Slickeen' and 'Zibermen'
TALK	'I'm gonna be killed by a Christmas tree!'

Pete Tyler married Jackie — and they had a daughter called Rose. Pete was always coming up with ideas of how to make money, everything from selling health drinks to marketing solar power panels, but nothing was ever very successful. When Rose was just a baby, Pete was hit by a car and died alone. Rose asked the Doctor to take her back to when her dad died, so she could be with him, but she saved him from the oncoming car and interfered with the time line. The action created a wound in time, and before it could be fixed Rose got the chance to meet her dad properly. When he realised how he could heal the wound, Pete gave up his life and everything was restored to normal. On a parallel Earth, Pete was a huge success and didn't die — and played a big part in fighting Cybermen.

Statistics

DEBUT	*Father's Day* (2005)
PLAYED BY	Shaun Dingwall
HOME	Earth
STATUS	Friend
HEIGHT	1.75m
SCARE RATING	Not applicable
SPECIAL FEATURES	Always coming up with unsuccessful schemes
WEAPONS	Not applicable
LIKES	His wife Jackie and daughter Rose
DISLIKES	Reapers, Cybermen
TALK	(To Rose) 'My eyes. Jackie's attitude. You sound like her when you shout.'

A boy genius, Adam Mitchell met the Doctor and Rose while he was working for the powerful and corrupt Henry Van Statten in an alien museum in Utah in the near future. When he was only eight, Adam managed to nearly cause a war by hacking into the US Department of Defense – just because he could. Unknown to Adam, deep inside the museum, Van Statten was holding something called a Dalek, one of the most evil creatures in the universe, as a prisoner. When the museum was shut down, the Doctor and Rose took Adam to see the stars, something he'd always wanted to do, in the TARDIS. But Adam abused his privileges and attempted to use knowledge from the future to make money when he got back to his own time. When the Doctor discovered this he was furious and returned the boy to this real home immediately.

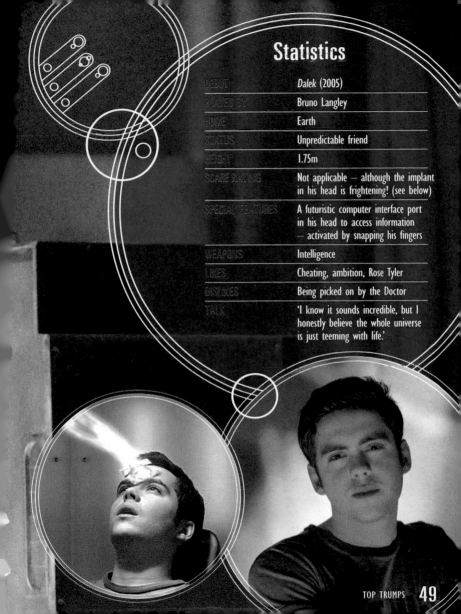

Statistics

DEBUT	*Dalek* (2005)
PLAYED BY	Bruno Langley
HOME	Earth
STATUS	Unpredictable friend
HEIGHT	1.75m
SCARE RATING	Not applicable — although the implant in his head is frightening! (see below)
SPECIAL FEATURES	A futuristic computer interface port in his head to access information — activated by snapping his fingers
WEAPONS	Intelligence
LIKES	Cheating, ambition, Rose Tyler
DISLIKES	Being picked on by the Doctor
TALK	'I know it sounds incredible, but I honestly believe the whole universe is just teeming with life.'

Harriet Jones
Prime Minister

Harriet Jones was the Member of
Parliament for Flydale North when she
became involved with the Doctor, Rose and
a corrupt alien family called the Slitheen.
She witnessed the murder of General
Asquith while hiding inside 10 Downing
Street and helped prevent the Slitheen from
destroying the Earth. A brave woman, she
went on to become the new Prime Minister.
While she was Prime Minister another alien
threat came to Earth – the Sycorax. In place
of the Queen's speech, Harriet put out a
plea on Christmas Day for the Doctor to
help them. She was relieved to see Rose
again and confused by the new face of the
regenerated Doctor. When the Sycorax
were leaving Earth she gave Torchwood
the order for their massive spaceship to
be destroyed. This act appalled the Doctor
and he lost all faith he had in Harriet Jones.
On the paralled Earth where the Doctor
defeated the Cybermen, Harriet Jones is the
President of Great Britain.

Statistics

DEBUT	*Aliens of London* (2005)
PLAYED BY	Penelope Wilton
HOME	London, England
STATUS	Friend
HEIGHT	1.70m
SCARE RATING	Not applicable
SPECIAL FEATURES	Intelligence
WEAPONS	Torchwood
LIKES	Cottage hosptials
DISLIKES	Alien threats
TALK	'Harriet Jones, Prime Minister...'

Charles Dickens is one the world's most famous writers. He wrote many books including *Oliver Twist*, *A Tale of Two Cities* and *Great Expectations*. The Doctor and Rose met Charles Dickens when they arrived in Cardiff on Christmas Eve 1869. Dickens was in Cardiff reading *A Christmas Carol* to a music hall audience when an old lady, who was dead and possessed by the alien gaseous Gelth, interrupted the performance. Dickens soon became caught up in the adventure – although he refused to believe in the alien creatures at first, thinking they were just a theatrical trick. He was able to rescue Rose and the Doctor from the attacking Gelth by gassing the creatures out of their bodies. The Doctor is a huge fan of Charles Dickens, although he did tell him that part of *Martin Chuzzlewit* was rubbish.

Statistics

DEBUT	*The Unquiet Dead* (2005)
PLAYED BY	Simon Callow
HOME	London
STATUS	Friend
HEIGHT	1.75m
SPACE TRAVEL	Not applicable
SPECIAL FEATURES	Eventually, open minded
WEAPONS	Not applicable
LIKES	Ghost stories, writing
DISLIKES	Being mocked, the Gelth

'All these huge and wonderful notions, Doctor! I'm inspired. I must write about them!'

AND COMPANY

DERTAKERS

PERANCE COURT

AND

Gwyneth
Servant girl

Gwyneth was an innocent, young servant girl who worked for Gabriel Sneed at his funeral parlour in Cardiff. She started working for him when she was twelve after her parents died. She grew up on top of the space/time rift, which gave her special powers. Gwyneth was able to see into people's minds and had second sight, a gift she had tried to understand but couldn't. She was forced into helping Sneed find the bodies that the Gelth were using, something she wasn't happy about. When Gwyneth met Rose she was able to see London in the future and told Rose that she had been thinking about her dead father more than ever, which shocked Rose. The Doctor asked the servant girl to help contact the Gelth, so she held a séance in the funeral parlour and the Gelth were able to communicate through her.

Statistics

DEBUT	*The Unquiet Dead* (2005)
PLAYED BY	Eve Myles
HOME	Cardiff, Wales
STATUS	Friend
HEIGHT	1.70m
SCARE RATING	Not applicable
SPECIAL FEATURES	Psychic
WEAPONS	Not applicable
LIKES	Angels
DISLIKES	Bodysnatching
TALK	'My mum said I had the sight. She told me to hide it!'

Reinette

Madame de Pompadour

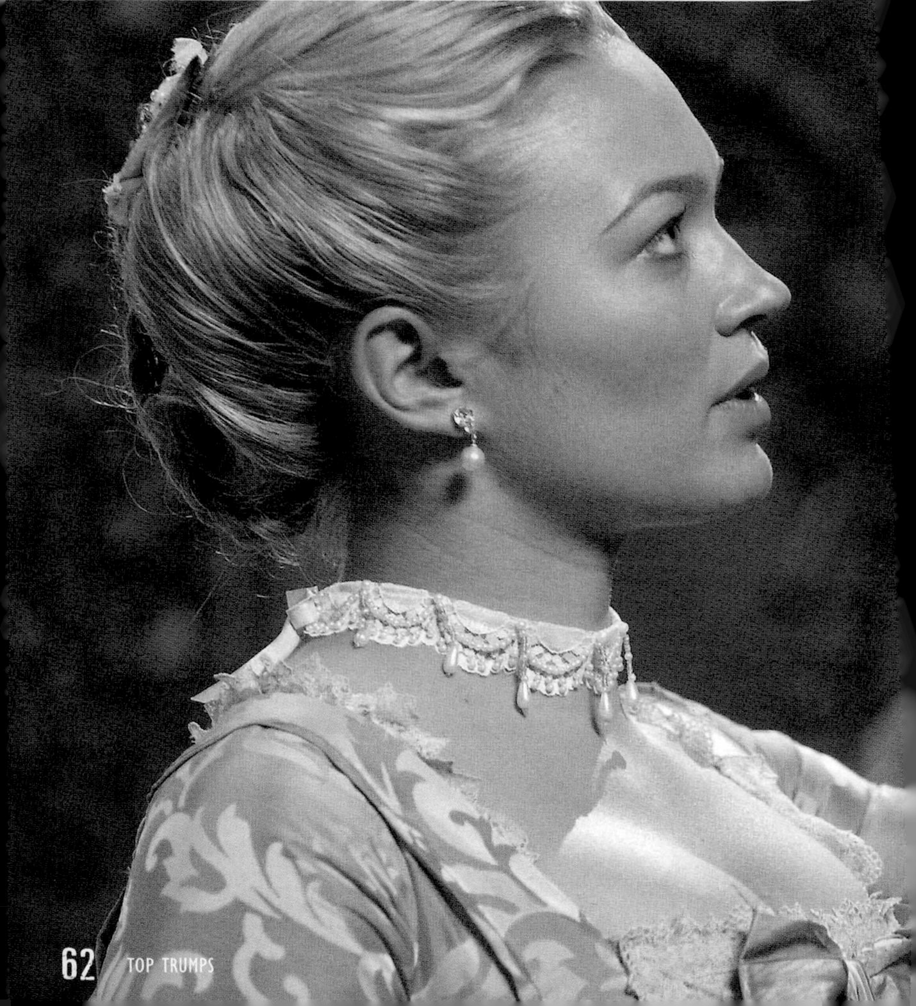

Because of confused and dangerous
Clockwork Robots, the beautiful
Reinette Poisson, also known as
Madame de Pompadour, knew
the Doctor all her life. He first
appeared to her on the other side
of a fireplace in her bedroom when
she was a young girl. The robots
opened up unstable time windows
into different parts of her life to find
a 37-year old Reinette. They wrongly
thought they could use her brain
to fix their damaged ship. Reinette
loved the Doctor and looked
forward to his many visits – although
whenever he appeared there was
always danger not far behind. The
Doctor nearly became trapped in
18th century France with Reinette,
but she was able to show the Doctor
an undamaged time window – her old
fireplace. The Doctor asked her to
come with him, but by the time he
returned through the window again
he was too late, as she had died.

Statistics

DEBUT	*The Girl in the Fireplace* (2006)
PLAYED BY	Sophia Myles
HOME	Paris, France
STATUS	Friend
HEIGHT	1.68m
SCARE RATING	Not applicable
SPECIAL FEATURES	Could see into the Doctor's mind
WEAPONS	Not applicable
LIKES	The Doctor — her 'fireplace man'
DISLIKES	Clockwork Robots
TALK	'The monsters and the Doctor. It seems you cannot have one without the other.'

The Face of Boe

Mysterious alien friend

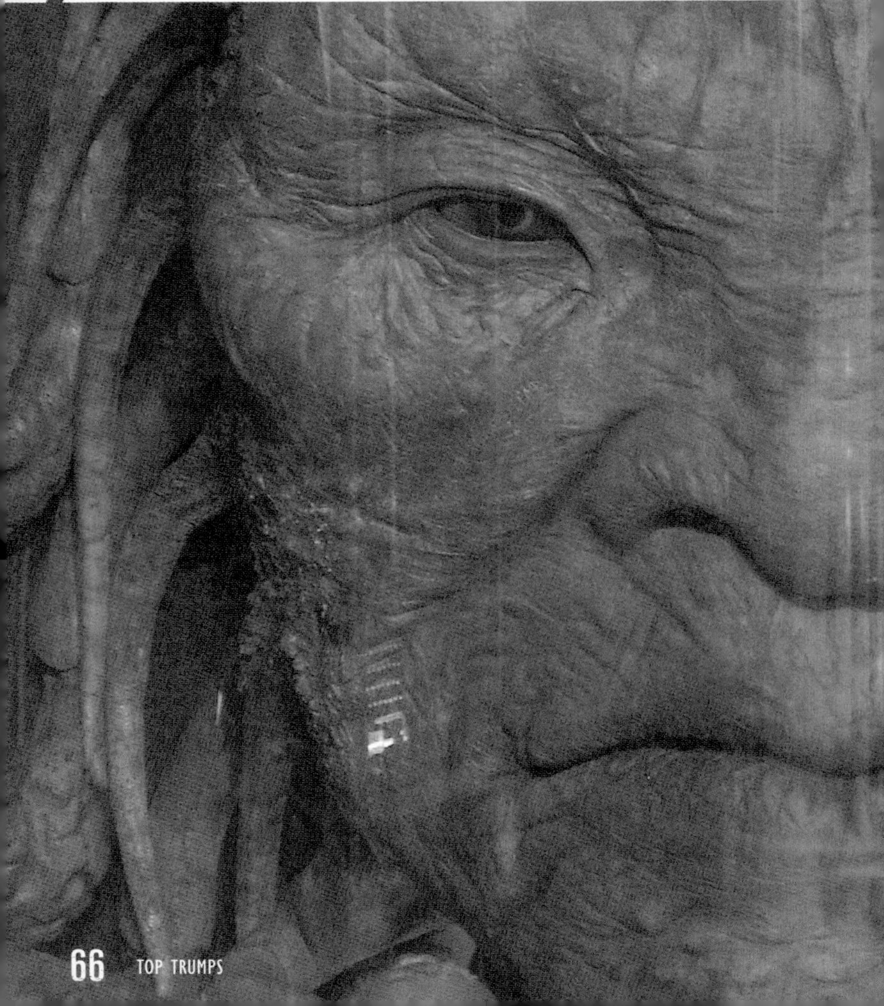

The Face of Boe

Mysterious alien friend

The Face of Boe is a friendly
alien that is, literally, a large
head contained in a tank. The
Face of Boe holds many secrets
and has lived forever. Legend
says that he has watched the
universe grow old – and he has
seen and heard many things
over the millions of years he has
been alive. The Doctor first met
Boe on Platform One when Boe
was the official sponsor for the
event that watched the Earth
explode in a ball of flames. Boe
met the Doctor again when he
projected a psychic message
across time asking the Doctor
to come to New Earth to visit
him in hospital, where he was
meant to be dying. He told the
Doctor that they will meet for a
third time – one final time – and
that just before his death he will
share his great secret.

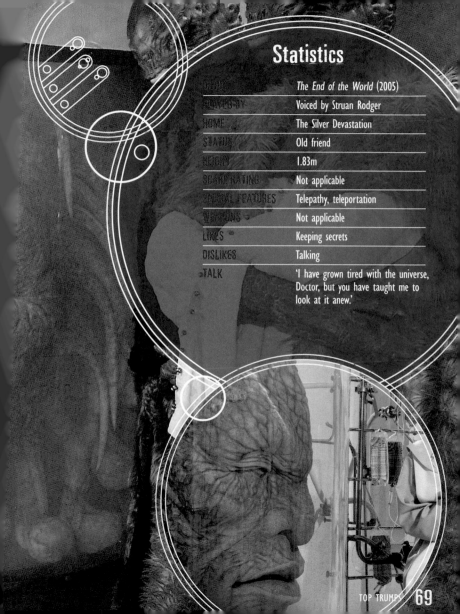

Statistics

DEBUT	*The End of the World* (2005)
PLAYED BY	Voiced by Struan Rodger
HOME	The Silver Devastation
STATUS	Old friend
HEIGHT	1.83m
SCARE RATING	Not applicable
SPECIAL FEATURES	Telepathy, teleportation
WEAPONS	Not applicable
LIKES	Keeping secrets
DISLIKES	Talking
TALK	'I have grown tired with the universe, Doctor, but you have taught me to look at it anew.'

The Moxx of Balhoon

Alien solicitor

The little blue Moxx of Balhoon joined Lady Cassandra and all the other wealthy guests on Platform One to watch the death of the planet Earth. Rose was shocked when the Moxx spat in her face as a form of welcome gift. An alien lawyer, he travelled around on a special anti-grav chair and represented Jolco and Jolco solicitors. With his sharp teeth and hard stare, the Moxx of Balhoon may have looked like an angry evil alien, but he was actually good. He was appalled to find out that robot spiders had infiltrated the whole of Platform One and demanded answers. He was keen for Lady Cassandra to be arrested when it was revealed that she was responsible for the chaos. As the temperature rose on Platform One, the Moxx, along with everyone else, panicked and later he died in the extreme heat.

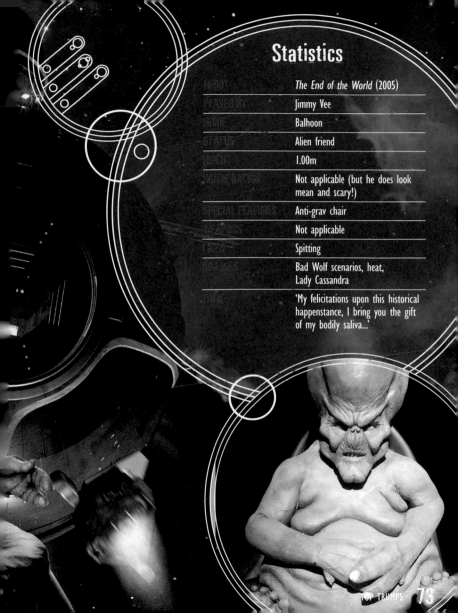

Statistics

DEBUT	*The End of the World* (2005)
PLAYED BY	Jimmy Vee
NAME	Balhoon
STATUS	Alien friend
HEIGHT	1.00m
SCARE RATING	Not applicable (but he does look mean and scary!)
SPECIAL FEATURES	Anti-grav chair
WEAPONS	Not applicable
LIKES	Spitting
DISLIKES	Bad Wolf scenarios, heat, Lady Cassandra
QUOTE	'My felicitations upon this historical happenstance, I bring you the gift of my bodily saliva...'

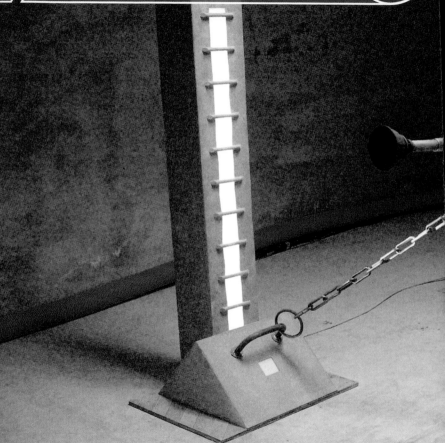

Daleks
Evil menace

The name Dalek is feared throughout the whole of the universe – and rightly so. The Daleks are the one monster that the Doctor is actually scared of. The virtually indestructible casing is a 'home' for an evil and ruthless mutated creature inside and gives the Dalek fantastic vision through its eyestalk and protection from the outside world and its enemies. The Daleks and the Doctor's people, the Time Lords, had a hideous war – the Time War – and it was thought that the race had died out. However, Daleks refuse to die! One fell back in time and ended up in an alien museum. The Emperor Dalek hid, and created a new race of Daleks from humans. And the Cult of Skaro kept millions of Daleks in the Genesis Ark. The Daleks always survive.

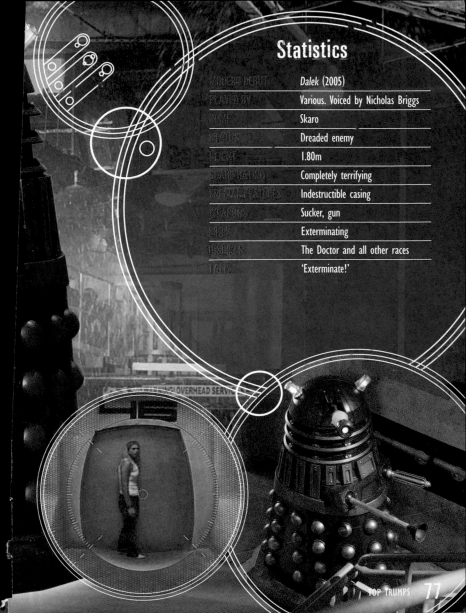

Statistics

MODERN DEBUT	*Dalek* (2005)
PLAYED BY	Various. Voiced by Nicholas Briggs
HOME	Skaro
STATUS	Dreaded enemy
HEIGHT	1.80m
SCARE RATING	Completely terrifying
SPECIAL FEATURES	Indestructible casing
WEAPONS	Sucker, gun
LIKES	Exterminating
DISLIKES	The Doctor and all other races
TALK	'Exterminate!'

Emperor Dalek

Supreme Dalek leader

Built into the biggest Dalek ship
of the fleet, the massive Emperor
Dalek, like all Daleks, hates all
other life other than Dalek life. His
ship survived the Time War, and
he was able to build up his empire
again using the human race to make
Daleks. Quite mad, the Emperor
called himself the god of all Daleks.
The Emperor taunted the ninth
Doctor as the Time Lord struggled
to defeat him with a Delta Wave
– which would have not only been
deadly to the Daleks but also to the
Earth. Rose turned up in the TARDIS,
having absorbed the Time Vortex,
and was able to put a stop to the
Dalek race (or so she thought). She
turned the Dalek Emperor and all his
Daleks into dust before the Doctor
was forced to save her from the
powers of the Time Vortex – which
made him regenerate.

Statistics

MODERN DEBUT	*The Parting of the Ways* (2005)
PLAYED BY	Voice of Nicholas Briggs
HOME	Skaro
STATUS	Enemy
HEIGHT	9.14m
SCARE RATING	Terrifying
SPECIAL FEATURES	Huge Dalek casing
WEAPONS	Army of Daleks
LIKES	Being a god, mass extermination of races
DISLIKES	The Doctor and Rose Tyler
QUOTE	'You destroyed us, Doctor. The Dalek race died in your inferno, but my ship survived, falling through time, crippled but alive.'

The Cult of Skaro

Secret group of Daleks

The Cult of Skaro

Secret group of Daleks

The Doctor thought the Cult of Skaro
was just a legend – but he was wrong!
A group of four Daleks that are more
autonomous than the Emperor Dalek,
they even have names. Dalek Thay,
Dalek Caan, Dalek Jast and Dalek Sec
the black Dalek appeared on Earth
in a void ship containing the Genesis
Ark. The Ark was a prison ship which
contained millions of angry, surviving
Daleks. The Cult's job was to think
like the enemy and come up with new
ways of exterminating them. They
had managed to escape the Time War
by hiding in the void ship between
universes. The ship came through
allowing the Cybermen to break into
our world – and when all the Daleks
inside the Ark awoke, it was soon war
on Earth between the two alien forces.
The Doctor opened the void and the
Daleks were pulled back into it – but
Dalek Sec, at least, escaped.

Statistics

DEBUT	*Doomsday (2006)*
PLAYED BY	Barnaby Edwards, Nicholas Pegg, Anthony Spargo, Dan Barratt, Dave Hankinson. Voiced by Nicholas Briggs
HOME	Skaro, originally
STATUS	Dangerous enemy
HEIGHT	1.80m
SCARE RATING	Terrifying
SPECIAL FEATURES	Indestructible casing, temporal shifting
WEAPONS	Sucker, gun
LIKES	Exterminating
DISLIKES	The void, the Doctor, all non-Dalek life
CATCHPHRASE	'This is not war. This is pest control.'

Cybermen

Powerful steel giants

Cybermen
Powerful steel giants

Like the Daleks, the Cybermen are one of the Doctor's oldest enemies. Emotionless, ruthless and deadly they are almost unstoppable in their urge to turn everyone into creatures like them – upgrading humans to what they believe is a better way of life to create a massive Cyber army. With all living tissue replaced with plastic and steel, these massive monsters have all their emotions removed from their brains with an emotional inhibitor. When the TARDIS fell into a parallel universe, the Doctor met a race of Cybermen that were being created by Cybus Industries – slightly different to the tall giants he'd met many times before. The Cybus Cybermen, created by a man called John Lumic, were even more dangerous and powerful – and it wasn't long before they worked out a way of breaking through into our world, wanting to upgrade the whole planet.

Statistics

MODERN DEBUT	*Rise of the Cybermen* (2006)
PLAYED BY	Various
HOME	Parallel Earth
STATUS	Powerful enemy
HEIGHT	2.15m
SCARE RATING	Terrifying
SPECIAL FEATURES	Emotionless
WEAPONS	Electronic shock through hands, laser bolt from arm
LIKES	Upgrading and the way they look
DISLIKES	Emotions, humans
TALK	'Delete!'

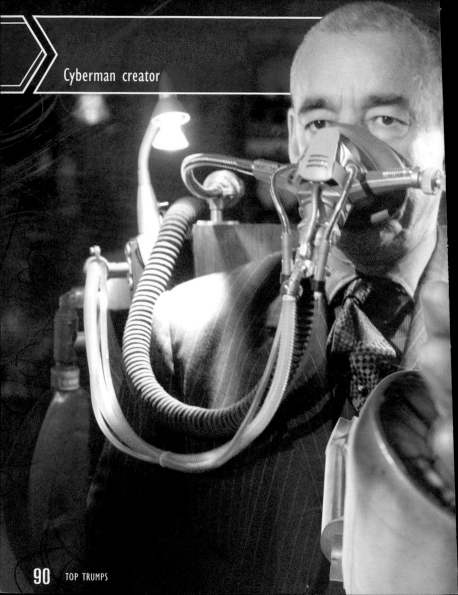

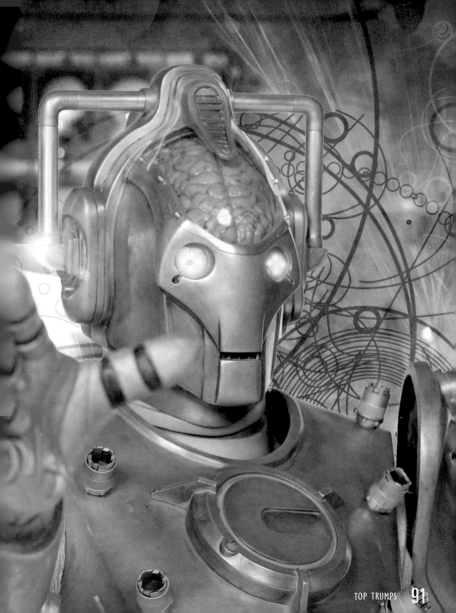

Cyber Controller

Cyberman creator

When John Lumic created the Cybermen, he didn't anticipate that his creations would turn against him and upgrade him in the way they did. Lumic was taken away to be upgraded, and returned as massive super Cyberman – the Cyber Controller. The Controller was wired into a throne with pipes that fed nutrients and power into his body. Looking almost like a regular Cyberman, the Controller's head is quite different – the normally protected brain of the original human is visible inside. When the Doctor managed to destroy most of the Cybermen in the Cyber factory in Battersea Power Station, the Controller ripped himself free from his throne and chased the Doctor, Rose and Pete to the rooftop and up a rope ladder to an escaping Zeppelin. With help from the Sonic Screwdriver, Pete was able to cut the ladder below him – and the Controller fell to his death.

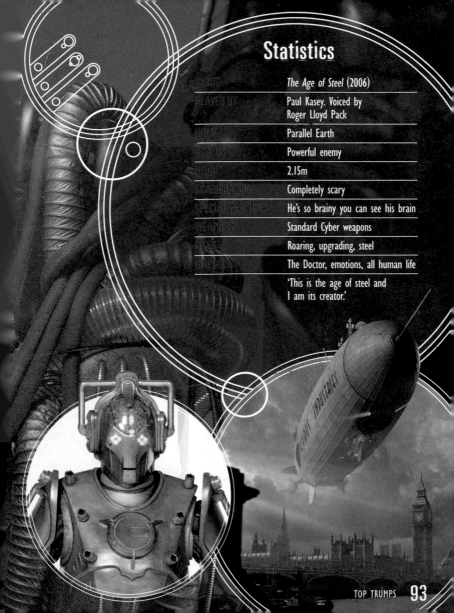

Statistics

DEBUT	*The Age of Steel* (2006)
PLAYED BY	Paul Kasey. Voiced by Roger Lloyd Pack
HOME	Parallel Earth
STATUS	Powerful enemy
HEIGHT	2.15m
SCARE RATING	Completely scary
SPECIAL FEATURES	He's so brainy you can see his brain
WEAPONS	Standard Cyber weapons
LIKES	Roaring, upgrading, steel
DISLIKES	The Doctor, emotions, all human life
	'This is the age of steel and I am its creator.'

Cyber Leaders

Cybermen with extra control

Troops of Cybermen are given a Cyber Leader
to manage their plans. Leaders can be spotted
by their black handles – more distinctive than
the regular Cyber creatures. It is not known
how many basic Cybermen report into the
Cyber Leaders, but basically they are Cybermen
with more power and the ability to make some
of the bigger Cyber decisions. In times of
emergency or if a Leader is destroyed, a regular
Cyberman can be upgraded to Leader – files can
be downloaded into the regular unit giving them
the same responsibilities as the former Leader.
A Cyber Leader broke through into Torchwood
Tower with all the other Cybermen – appearing
like ghosts along with other Cyber figures when
Torchwood opened the void. This Leader was
destroyed when Pete Tyler, Jake and members of
the Resistance followed them through.

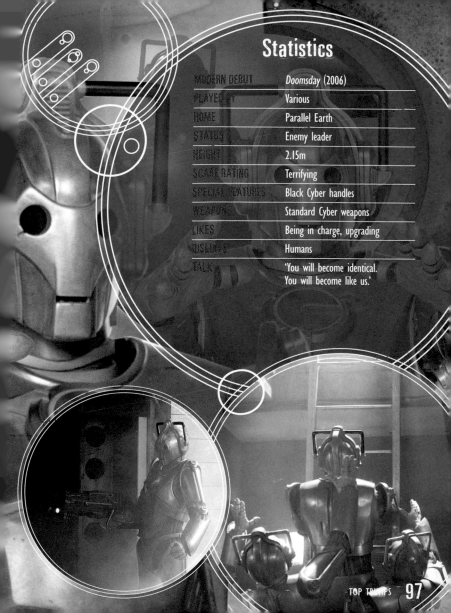

Statistics

MODERN DEBUT	*Doomsday* (2006)
PLAYED BY	Various
HOME	Parallel Earth
STATUS	Enemy leader
HEIGHT	2.15m
SCARE RATING	Terrifying
SPECIAL FEATURES	Black Cyber handles
WEAPONS	Standard Cyber weapons
LIKES	Being in charge, upgrading
DISLIKES	Humans
TALK	'You will become identical. You will become like us.'

Autons
Living Plastic creatures

The Autons, also known as Living Plastic, are the silent plastic monstrosities controlled by the Nestene Consciousness. We don't know what planet the Nestene come from, but what we do know is that they've attempted to take over the Earth several times by turning all types of plastic into deadly weapons. The result? Shop window dummies that kill and wheelie bins that swallow people whole. Most recently, when the food stocks of the Nestene Consciousness were destroyed after the Time War, the massive alien Nestene came to Earth to feed on all the toxins that can be found there. It's the perfect food supply for the creature. The Autons were the first alien creatures that Rose Tyler encountered. Deep in the basement of the shop she worked in, a group of shop dummies followed her and were about to attack her – but then the Doctor appeared...

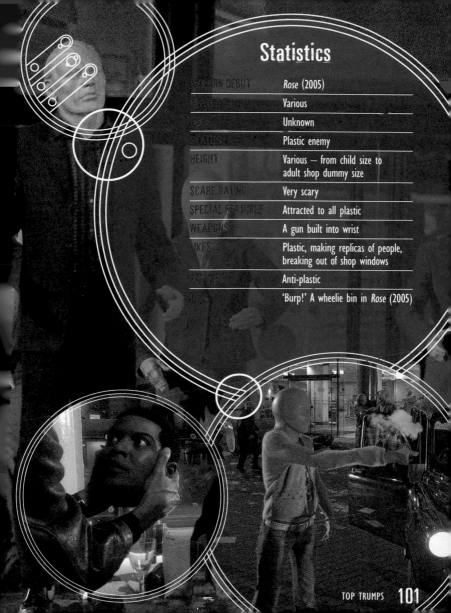

Statistics

SCREEN DEBUT	*Rose* (2005)
PLANET	Various
DATE	Unknown
STATUS	Plastic enemy
HEIGHT	Various — from child size to adult shop dummy size
SCARE RATING	Very scary
SPECIAL FEATURES	Attracted to all plastic
WEAPONS	A gun built into wrist
LIKES	Plastic, making replicas of people, breaking out of shop windows
DISLIKES	Anti-plastic
	'Burp!' A wheelie bin in *Rose* (2005)

Cassandra

The last surviving human

When the Doctor and Rose first met Lady Cassandra O'Brien Dot Delta Seventeen it was the year five billion and the Earth was about to die. The last surviving pure Human, Cassandra is a piece of stretched skin in a special frame that also houses her brain. She attempted to sabotage Platform One in order to con insurance and ransom money out of her fellow guests – the money would help her pay for her very expensive surgery that kept her looking gorgeous. The Doctor managed to stop her, and left Cassandra to dry out, explode and die. However, years later, Cassandra was discovered beneath a hospital on New Earth. Her brain and body parts had survived and she had been put back together with extra skin from her old body. This time her plan was to use a psychograft machine to leave her brain and body behind. The first body she chose was Rose's.

Statistics

DEBUT	*The End of the World* (2005)
PLAYED BY	Computer generated and Zoë Wanamaker
HOME	Earth
STATUS	Enemy
HEIGHT	1.77m
SCARE RATING	Scary lady!
SPECIAL FEATURES	She's a piece of stretched skin
WEAPONS	Psychograft, poison perfume, moisturiser, robot spiders
LIKES	Keeping her looks
DISLIKES	Dry skin, heat, getting old, Rose ('dirty blonde assassin!'), chavs
TALK	'Moisturise me!'

Chip

Cassandra's servant

Chip is Cassandra's servant – she calls him her pet. He's not a proper life-form but a force-grown clone. Faithful to his mistress, he sees to all her needs and looked after her in the basement of the hospital on New Earth for a long time. When he and Cassandra lured Rose down into the basement, he helped Cassandra with the pyschograft machine, allowing Cassandra to enter Rose's brain and mind so his lady could be free. Chip eventually gave up his own life willingly so that Cassandra could use his body. But Chip's body was dying, so the Doctor, taking pity on Cassandra, took her back to a time when was still looked like a human and allowed 'Chip' as Cassandra to tell her that she looked beautiful. Chip's body died soon after.

Statistics

DEBUT	*New Earth* (2006)
PLAYED BY	Sean Gallagher
HOME	New Earth
STATUS	Enemy servant
HEIGHT	1.70m
SUPERPOWER	Not applicable
SPECIAL FEATURES	Patterned face
WEAPONS	Psychograft machine
LIKES	Lady Cassandra
DISLIKES	Scary situations
TALK	'I worship the mistress!'

Robot Spiders

Murderous robots

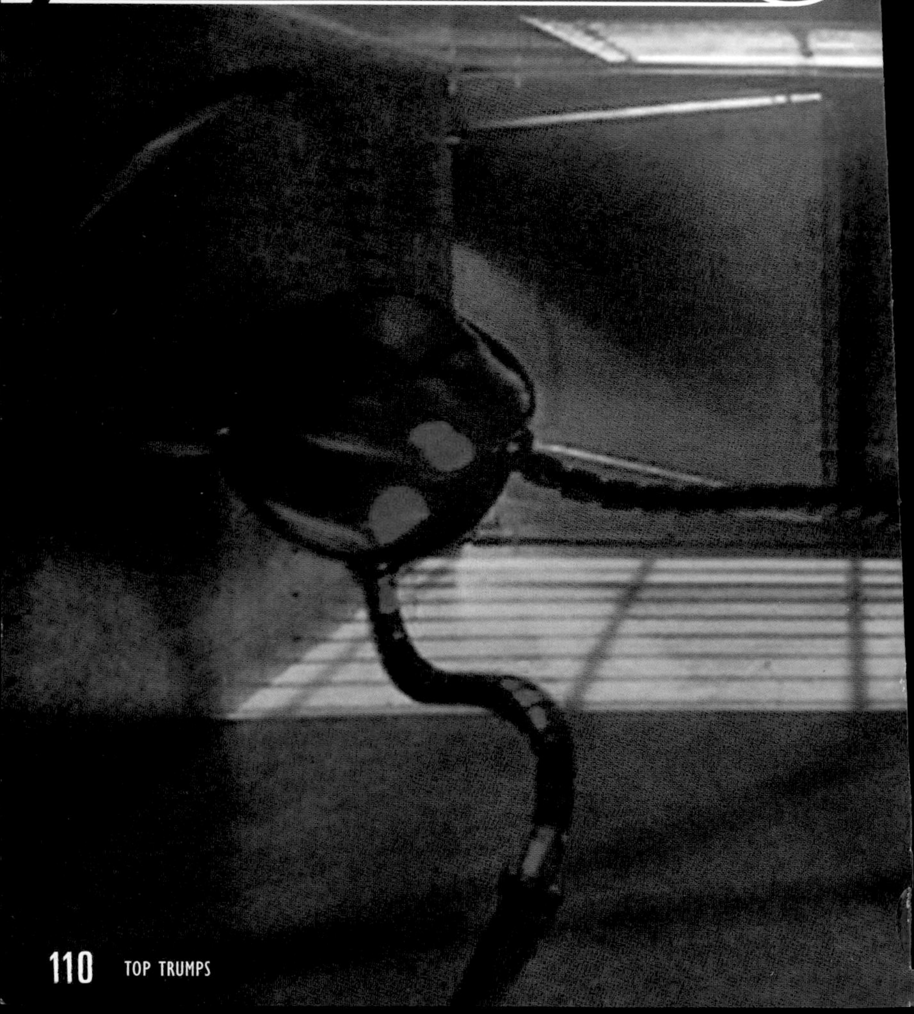

Robot Spiders
Murderous robots

Disguised as silver spheres, the robot spiders were controlled by the scheming Lady Cassandra. Cassandra's other servants, the Adherents of the Repeated Meme, handed out the spheres to the many guests on Platform One as 'a gift of peace'. The spheres slipped through the various security channels as they had been carried aboard as presents. When they couldn't be seen, the spiders activated. Out popped four very strong legs allowing them to scuttle off to hide in the ducts and damage parts of the platform. The spiders were able to attack a young female plumber by pulling her into the ducts and they also opened up the sunfilter in the Steward's office – killing him instantly. On Cassandra's command, the spiders were ordered to explode and destroy the safety systems on Platform One. With the force-fields gone there would be no protection from the exploding planet.

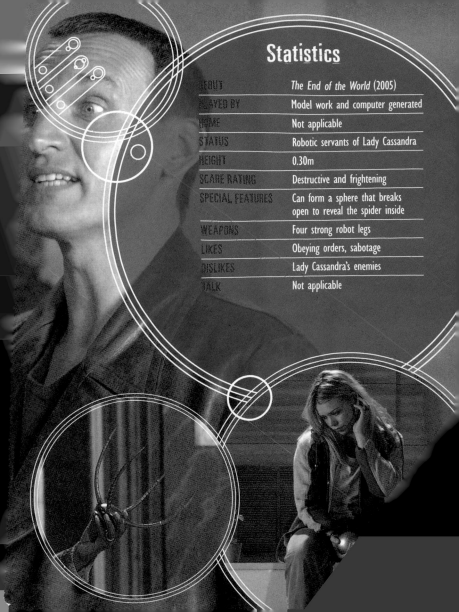

Statistics

DEBUT	*The End of the World* (2005)
PLAYED BY	Model work and computer generated
HOME	Not applicable
STATUS	Robotic servants of Lady Cassandra
HEIGHT	0.30m
SCARE RATING	Destructive and frightening
SPECIAL FEATURES	Can form a sphere that breaks open to reveal the spider inside
WEAPONS	Four strong robot legs
LIKES	Obeying orders, sabotage
DISLIKES	Lady Cassandra's enemies
TALK	Not applicable

Strange cloaked figures

From Financial Family Seven, or so they said, the cloaked Adherents of the Repeated Meme arrived on Platform One along with the Moxx of Balhoon, Lady Cassandra, the Forest of Cheem and various other guests to watch the Earth die in a ball of flames millions of years from now. They were one of the first alien races that Rose met when she started travelling with the Doctor. The Adherents would recite their meme every thirty minutes. We don't see much of their features, apart from a long, powerful metal arm. It turned out that the Adherents were actually remote-controlled androids being used by Lady Cassandra to distribute robotic spiders amongst the guests to cause chaos on Platform One. When the Doctor ripped off one of their arms, all the Adherents collapsed – and Cassandra was revealed as a murderer.

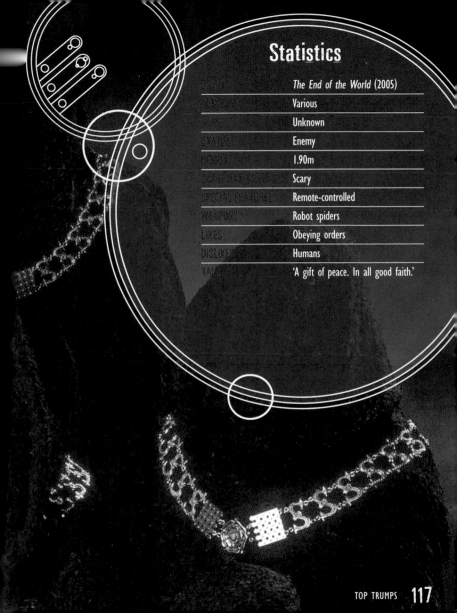

Statistics

FROM	*The End of the World* (2005)
PLANET	Various
NAME	Unknown
STATUS	Enemy
HEIGHT	1.90m
SCARE RATING	Scary
SPECIAL FEATURES	Remote-controlled
WEAPONS	Robot spiders
LIKES	Obeying orders
DISLIKES	Humans
TALK	'A gift of peace. In all good faith.'

Descendants from the tropical rainforests on Earth, the Forest of Cheem are a group of friendly and elegant tree people. They have forests all over the universe. Three members of the Forest – Jabe, Lute and Coffa – arrived on Platform One to witness the end of the Earth. Jabe took a big interest in the Doctor – and was surprised to find out he was a Time Lord, a race she knew about and thought had all perished in the great Time War. Jabe gave the Doctor a small cutting of her grandfather as a token of friendship. In return he gave her air from his lungs, a gesture Jabe found very intimate. Jabe helped the Doctor save Platform One from destruction when Cassandra attempted to sabotage the event – and gave up her life while doing so. She caught fire as heat levels rose on the Platform.

Statistics

DEBUT	*The End of the World* (2005)
PLAYED BY	Yasmin Bannerman, Paul Kasey, Alan Ruscoe
HOME	Originally from Earth
STATUS	Friends
HEIGHT	1.78m
SCARE RATING	Not applicable
SPECIAL FEATURES	Can use their vines to catch things
WEAPONS	Not appliable
LIKES	Nature
DISLIKES	Heat
TALK	Jabe: 'So many species evolved from that planet. Mankind is only one. I'm another.'

Gelth

Bodysnatching gas aliens

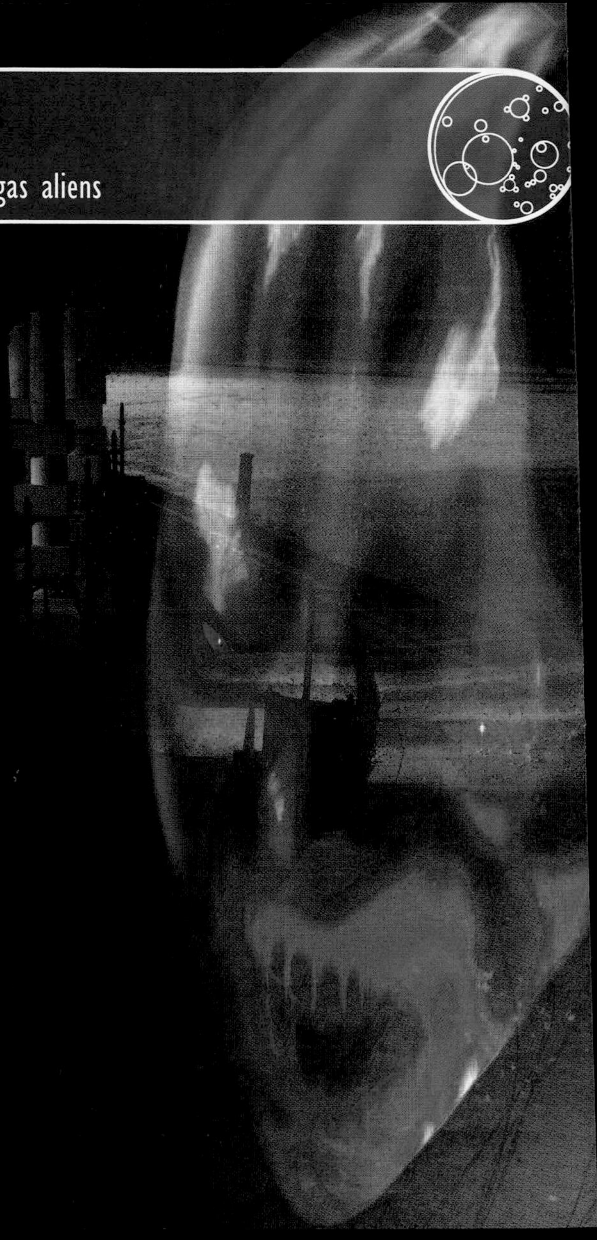

Gelth

Bodysnatching gas aliens

The Gelth tricked the Doctor into helping them. The alien Gelth had no bodies of their own and took over dead bodies so they could walk again. Gaseous ghost-like creatures, the Gelth came to Earth through a rift in the space/time continuum, which, conveniently, was situated in an undertaker's in Victorian Cardiff – perfect for bodysnatching! When the Doctor discovered that the Gelth had lost their bodies as a result of the Time War and that they were nearly extinct, he decided to help them. But the Gelth lied to the Doctor – there were billions of them waiting to come through the rift and they wanted to kill humans so that they could all have new bodies. A young servant girl called Gwyneth thought the Gelth were angels. She created a bridge for them to come through and, to save the world, she blew up the rift trapping the Gelth in the other world.

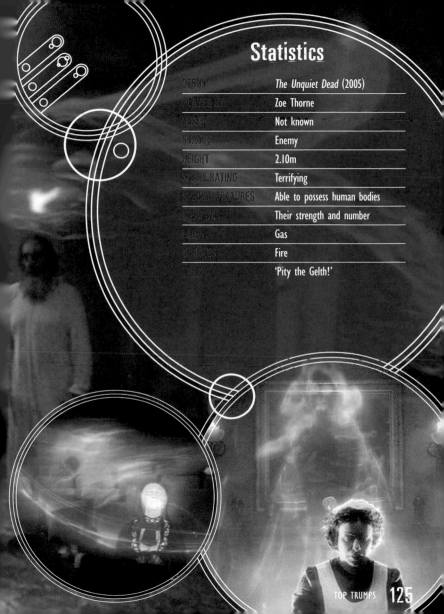

Statistics

DEBUT	*The Unquiet Dead* (2005)
APPEARED AS	Zoe Thorne
HOME	Not known
STATUS	Enemy
HEIGHT	2.10m
SCARE RATING	Terrifying
SPECIAL FEATURES	Able to possess human bodies
WEAPONS	Their strength and number
LIKES	Gas
DISLIKES	Fire
QUOTE	'Pity the Gelth!'

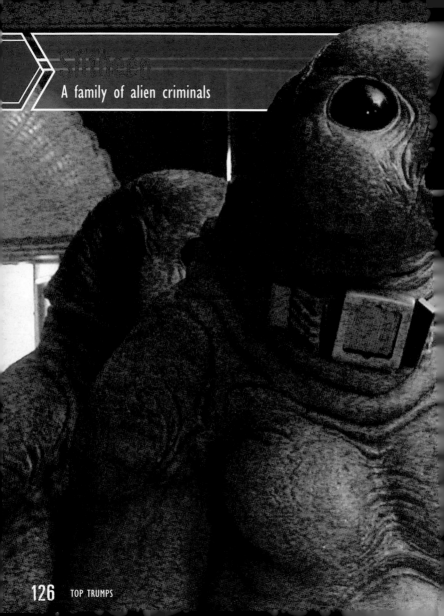

Slitheen

A family of alien criminals

Slitheen

A family of alien criminals

The slimy, farting Slitheen are a large criminal family from Raxacoricofallapatorius. Through clever technology, they have the ability to compress their massive alien bodies down so that they can fit inside a human skin – the perfect disguise for invading Earth. However, one side effect is a farting sound brought about by a gas exchange. The Slitheen enjoy hunting and business – and they came to Earth intending to start a nuclear war. They even managed to get inside 10 Downing Street, where the Prime Minister lives, and fake an alien crash in London. If the Earth was reduced to radioactive waste the Slitheen could sell it on and make a great deal of money. The Doctor, along with Rose and Harriet Jones, prevented the alien family from causing a war and blew up Number 10 to save the world. One Slitheen – 'Margaret' Slitheen – escaped and moved to Cardiff to become Mayor.

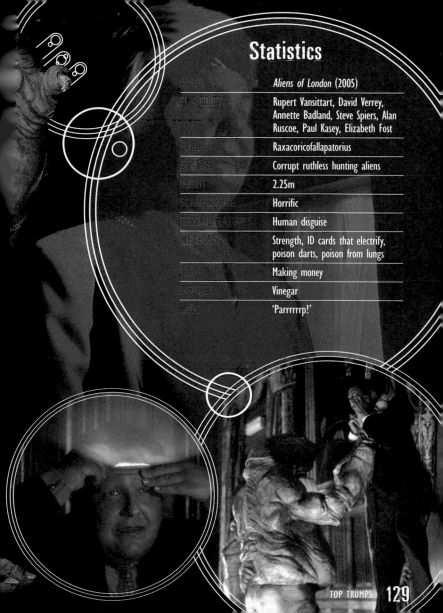

Statistics

DEBUT	*Aliens of London* (2005)
PLAYED BY	Rupert Vansittart, David Verrey, Annette Badland, Steve Spiers, Alan Ruscoe, Paul Kasey, Elizabeth Fost
HOME	Raxacoricofallapatorius
STATUS	Corrupt ruthless hunting aliens
HEIGHT	2.25m
SCARE RATING	Horrific
SPECIAL FEATURES	Human disguise
WEAPONS	Strength, ID cards that electrify, poison darts, poison from lungs
LIKES	Making money
DISLIKES	Vinegar
TALK	'Parrrrrrp!'

The Jagrafess

The boss of Satellite Five

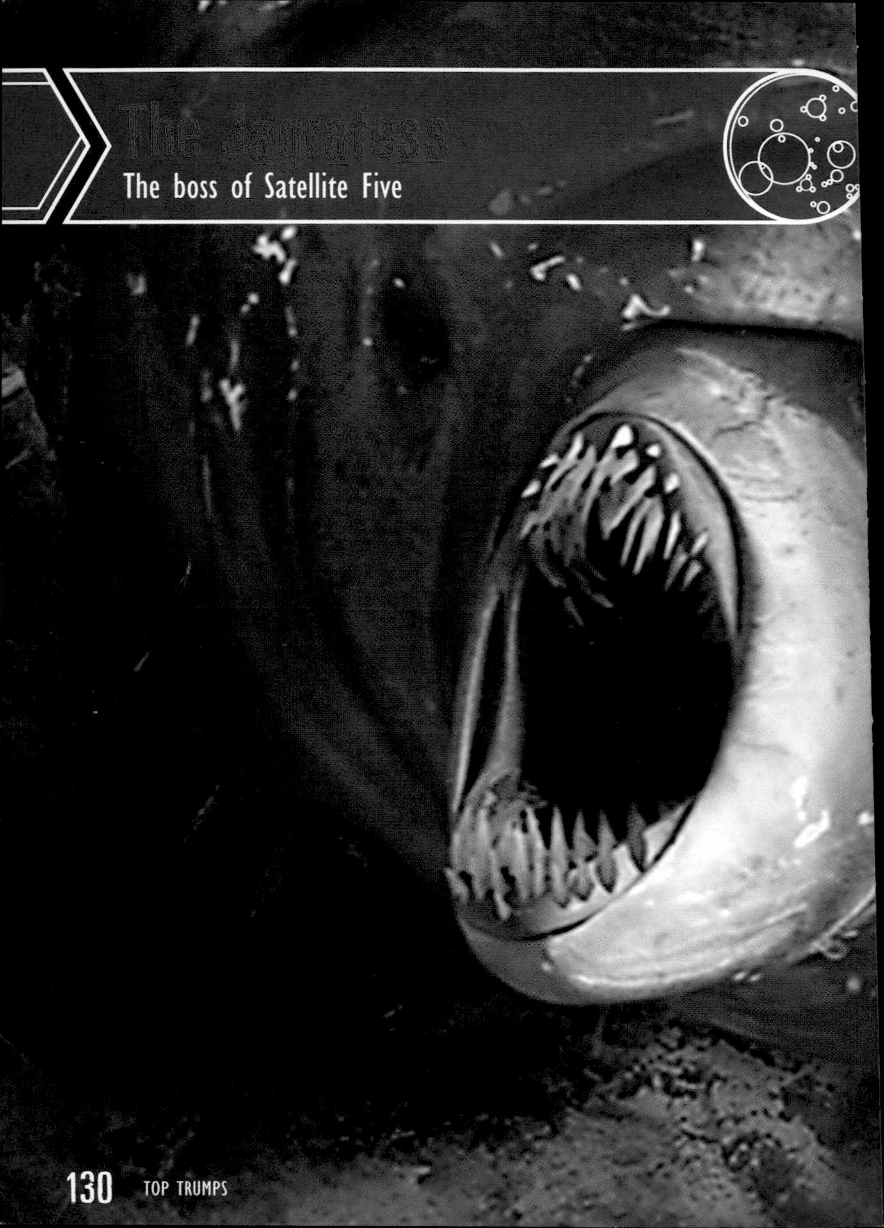

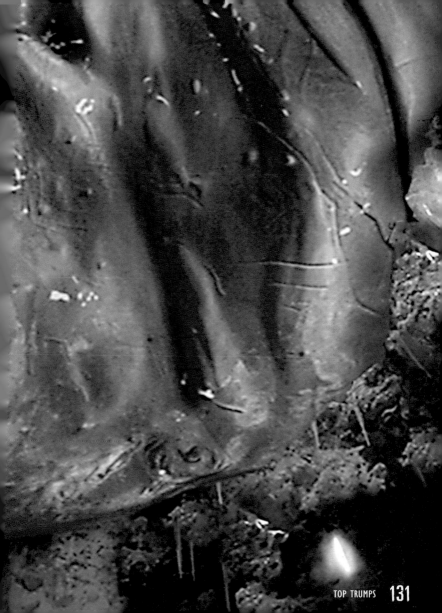

The Jagrafess

The boss of Satellite Five

In the Fourth Great and Bountiful Human Empire, the Mighty Jagrafess of the Holy Hadrojassic Maxarodenfoe was a massive, horrific creature that lived at the top of Satellite Five for nearly 100 years. The slavering creature had a load of sharp teeth and liked to roar when things didn't go as planned. The nightmarish monster was put on the satellite by a number of banks to control broadcasting across the Empire. This corrupt creature, with the help of the Editor, managed to influence events to make money for the banks. The Jagrafess needed cool temperatures to survive, so the top floor of Satellite Five was icy cold. Just as the Doctor and Rose were about to be eaten by the monster, a journalist called Cathica managed to turn up the heating on the top floor, causing the monster to swell up, overheat and explode everywhere.

Statistics

DEBUT	*The Long Game* (2005)
PLAYED BY	Computer generated
HOME	Satellite Five
STATUS	Big alien monster
HEIGHT	3.10m
SCARE RATING	The size alone is terrifying
SPECIAL FEATURES	Rows of sharp teeth
WEAPONS	None visible — but uses the Editor to carry out his dirty work
LIKES	Roaring, being in control and shaping Mankind...
DISLIKES	Heat
TALK	'Roooar!'

The Editor

Corrupt employee of the Jagrafess

On Floor 500, at the top of Satellite Five above Earth, the evil white-haired Editor controls a very corrupt broadcasting station. Every news broadcast was being manipulated to create fear and hate around the Empire. The Editor represented a number of banks and he could make lots of money for them by interfering with the news broadcasts. He was able to patch into the thoughts of journalists who had special chips inside their head – making him a very powerful and dangerous man. When Adam Mitchell had an operation to have a chip inserted, the Editor was able to discover that the Doctor was a Time Lord and he had a TARDIS. But even worse than the Editor is his boss – the gigantic slavering creature known as the Mighty Jagrafess of the Holy Hadrojassic Maxarodenfoe. Or, as the Editor liked to called him, Max.

Statistics

DEBUT	*The Long Game* (2005)
PLAYED BY	Simon Pegg
HOME	Earth
STATUS	Enemy editor
HEIGHT	1.78m
SCARE RATING	Scary
SPECIAL FEATURES	Pale skin, white hair
WEAPONS	The Jagrafess
LIKES	Pleasing the Jagrafess, the cold, news, money
DISLIKES	Liars, journalists
TAG	'Today, we are the headlines. We can rewrite history. We could prevent mankind from ever developing.'

Reapers
Time predators

The Reapers live off wounds in time. They take it upon themselves to fix any problem in time by devouring people whole. They are frighteningly powerful and virtually unstoppable – and will attack anyone or anything that gets in the way. The Time Lords used to watch out for the Reapers' behaviour, but after the Time War the Reapers were left to do whatever they wanted. Rose Tyler brought the Reapers into our world when she saved her dad from a car accident, massively disrupting time. It wasn't long before the large winged creatures turned up and started eating everyone. The Reapers didn't go away until Pete realised he was causing all the destruction. He ran out in front of the car that was meant to have killed him, was knocked down dead, and the Reapers disappeared.

Statistics

DEBUT	*Father's Day* (2005)
PLAYED BY	Computer generated
HOME	Anywhere there's a wound in time
STATUS	Enemy
HEIGHT	2.80m
SCARE RATING	The stuff of nightmares
SPECIAL FEATURES	Flight
WEAPONS	Sharp claws and can swallow people whole
LIKES	Sterilising wounds
DISLIKES	Faults in time
TALK	'Screeeeech!'

Gas-mask zombie

In London during the Blitz, 1941, a child with a gas mask is terrorising the whole city. And it appears he has lost his mummy. Young Jamie's touch will turn everyone he comes into contact with into a gas-masked version of himself. The child manages to communicate through all types of equipment – everything from a typewriter to the telephone stored inside the police box door of the TARDIS. When a Chula medical ship crashed in London, special medical nanogenes on board the ship tried to repair Jamie's damaged body – not recognising his form, they thought his gas-masked body was what humans should look like so attempted to 'cure' everyone. When the child eventually comes into contact with his mother, a young girl called Nancy, the intelligent nanogenes are able to undo the damage they had done. And everyone is returned to normal.

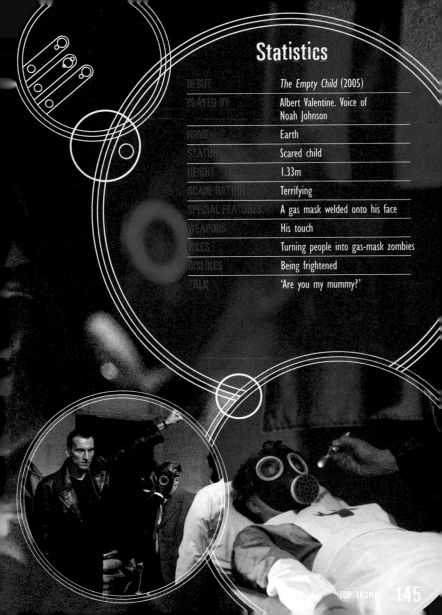

Statistics

DEBUT	*The Empty Child* (2005)
PLAYED BY	Albert Valentine. Voice of Noah Johnson
HOME	Earth
STATUS	Scared child
HEIGHT	1.33m
SCARE RATING	Terrifying
SPECIAL FEATURES	A gas mask welded onto his face
WEAPONS	His touch
LIKES	Turning people into gas-mask zombies
DISLIKES	Being frightened
TALK	'Are you my mummy?'

Misguided cat nuns

The Sisters of Plenitude are cat-like nuns who run a hospital on New Earth in the far future. The Sisters made a life-long vow to help others and heal the sick. But you should never trust a cat, as the old Earth saying goes. The Sisters had a rather nasty secret. To cure people, they bred humans deep beneath the hospital so they could infect them with all known diseases. When the Doctor and Rose appeared on New Earth they discovered the secret of the Sisters' medical success – as did Lady Cassandra who'd been watching them for some time. Cassandra wanted to blackmail them so their secret remained safe. When Matron Casp refused Cassandra's terms, Cassandra released the 'patients' into the open and suddenly everyone they touched died instantly. After the Doctor cured the patients the New New York Police Department arrested all of the sisters who were still alive.

Statistics

DEBUT	*New Earth* (2006)
PLAYED BY	Dona Croll, Adjoa Andoh, Anna Hope
HOME	New Earth
STATUS	Cat nuns with bad moral attitude
HEIGHT	1.73m
SCARE RATING	Scary if you don't like cats
SPECIAL FEATURES	Can cure people of every known disease
WEAPONS	Sharp claws
LIKES	Treating patients
DISLIKES	Being answerable for their actions
TALK	'Who needs arms, when we have claws!'

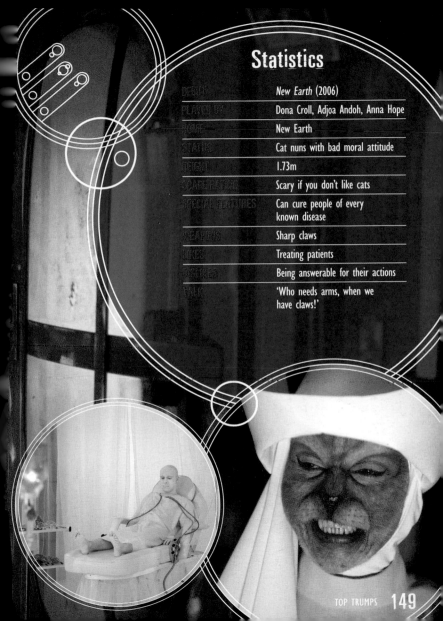

Sycorax

Bone-faced warriors

Sycorax
Bone-faced warriors

Bold, bony and loud, these alien warrior monsters trick planets into surrendering – and almost succeeded in capturing the Earth one Christmas. Travelling long distances in massive stone spaceships they use blood control to hypnotise planets into giving up their people and world. Their horrific bodies have no skin, and their faces are usually hidden beneath a bone helmet. They are ruled by one Leader, the strongest Sycorax of them all. While the Doctor was recovering from his regeneration, Rose took it upon herself to confront the Sycorax Leader and asked him to go away. He laughed at her attempt – he thought she was very funny, indicating that Sycorax appreciate humour. Luckily, the Doctor recovered in time to have a sword fight with the Sycorax Leader and won. He ordered them to leave, and as they did, Harriet Jones gave the order for them to be blown out of the sky.

Statistics

DEBUT	*The Christmas Invasion* (2005)
PLAYED BY	Leader played by Sean Gilder
HOME	An asteroid far away
STATUS	Bone-faced enemy
HEIGHT	1.91m
SCARE RATING	Terror at Christmas time!
SPECIAL FEATURES	Bone helmets
WEAPONS	Swords, whips and blood control
USES	Controlling people with blood, combat, war
DISLIKES	The English language
TALK	'Sycorax rock!'

Pilot Fish

Scavenging aliens

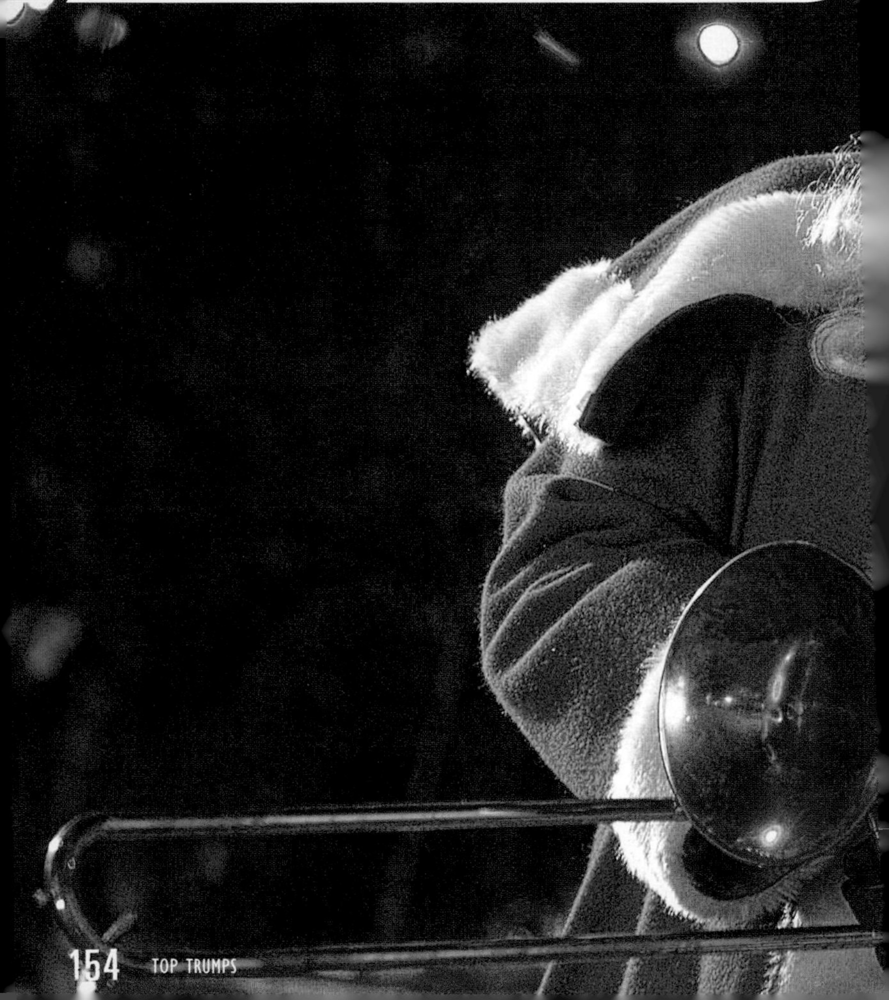

The Pilot Fish are scavenging robots that scour the universe ahead of bigger and more dangerous threats. They disguise themselves so they don't stand out – so when they arrived on Earth prior to the Sycorax invasion one Christmas, they adopted a festive disguise and they looked like Santa Clauses. The Pilot Fish wanted the Doctor, and decided to get rid of people around him. As Rose and Mickey did some last-minute Christmas shopping, the Pilot Fish sensed the energy from the Doctor's regeneration on Rose, and tried to kill the pair by firing at them with their trombone flame-thrower weapons, completely destroying a Christmas market. Meanwhile, more Pilot Fish had delivered a dangerous killer Christmas tree to Jackie's flat – and Rose and Mickey returned to rescue her just in time. The tree activated and cut through Jackie's door and walls, until the Doctor stopped it with his sonic screwdriver.

Statistics

DEBUT	*The Christmas Invasion* (2005)
PLAYED BY	Various
HOME	Unknown
STATUS	Scavenging enemy
HEIGHT	1.83m
SCARE RATING	Sinister and scary
SPECIAL FEATURES	Santa disguise
WEAPONS	Trombone flame throwers, violent Christmas trees
LIKES	Christmas scares
DISLIKES	The Doctor
TALK	Silent robots, although they can play musical instruments

The Werewolf
Howling alien

The werewolf was an alien creature that fell to Earth, landing in Scotland in 1540 near a monastery in the Glen of St Catherine. Over the next 300 years the creature gathered strength and evolved into something that could steal human bodies. The alien needed a host body so it could walk on the Earth and turn into a howling, slavering werewolf whenever there was a full moon. The werewolf could be heard howling throughout the valley, and stories of the wolf were rife in that part of Scotland – especially when animals were found dead the next morning. The Doctor called the creature a lupine wavelength haemovariform – and he thought it was beautiful, however deadly it was. With the help of Father Angelo and his brethren of monks, the werewolf planned to infect Queen Victoria so she could become the next Host.

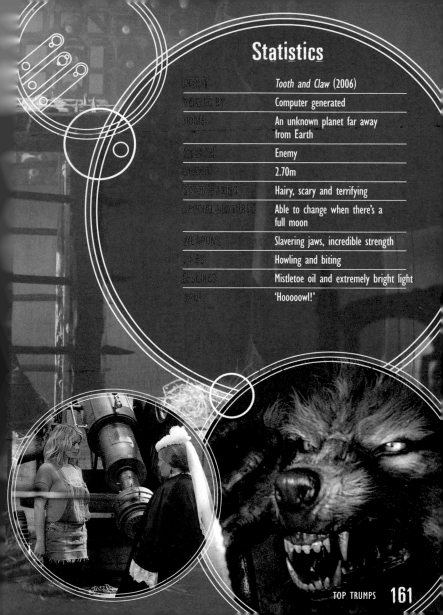

Statistics

DEBUT	*Tooth and Claw* (2006)
PLAYED BY	Computer generated
HOME	An unknown planet far away from Earth
FRIEND	Enemy
HEIGHT	2.70m
SCARE RATING	Hairy, scary and terrifying
SPECIAL ABILITIES	Able to change when there's a full moon
WEAPONS	Slavering jaws, incredible strength
LIKES	Howling and biting
DISLIKES	Mistletoe oil and extremely bright light
SAYS	'Hooooowl!'

Confused droids

The beautifully designed clockwork droids were repair robots on a spaceship called *The Madame de Pompadour* in the 51st century. Being clockwork meant that they could still work if the ship was damaged or there was a power failure. When the ship ran into an ion storm the droids started to repair the ship with body parts of the crew. Using their own form of logic, the confused droids thought that they needed a vital part to fix the ship, though – the brain of a 37-year-old Madame de Pomapdour, also known as Reinette Poisson. In order to track her down, they opened time windows into the past and searched throughout Reinette's life in 18th century France until they found her at the correct age. To blend in, they wore elegant costumes, wigs and masks from that time.

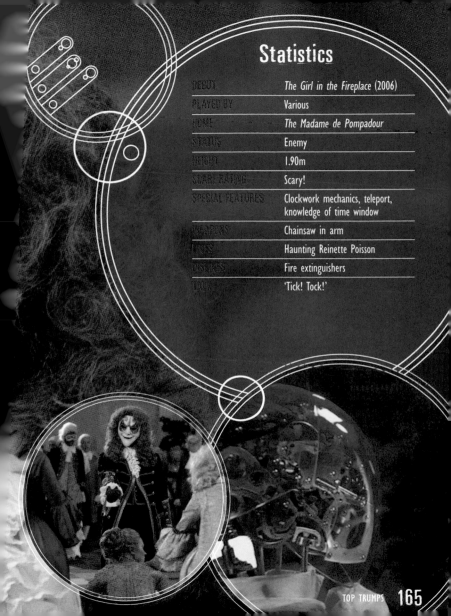

Statistics

DEBUT	*The Girl in the Fireplace* (2006)
PLAYED BY	Various
HOME	*The Madame de Pompadour*
STATUS	Enemy
HEIGHT	1.90m
SCARE RATING	Scary!
SPECIAL FEATURES	Clockwork mechanics, teleport, knowledge of time window
WEAPONS	Chainsaw in arm
LIKES	Haunting Reinette Poisson
DISLIKES	Fire extinguishers
TALK	'Tick! Tock!'

Harriet Jones
Date   Comments

Charles Dickens
Date   Comments

Gwyneth
Date   Comments

Reinette
Date   Comments

The Face of Boe
Date   Comments

The Moxx of Balhoon
Date   Comments

Daleks
Date   Comments

Emperor Dalek
Date   Comments

The Cult of Skaro
Date   Comments

Cybermen
Date   Comments

Cyber Controller
Date   Comments

Cyber Leaders
Date   Comments

Autons
Date   Comments

Cassandra
Date   Comments

Chip
Date   Comments

Robot Spiders
Date   Comments

Adherents of the Repeated Meme
Date   Comments

Forest of Cheem
Date   Comments

Gelth
Date   Comments

Slitheen
Date   Comments

The Jagrafess
Date   Comments

The Editor
Date   Comments

Reapers
Date   Comments

The Empty Child
Date   Comments

Sisters of Plenitude
Date   Comments

Sycorax
Date   Comments

Pilot Fish
Date   Comments

The Werewolf
Date   Comments

Clockwork Robots
Date   Comments

Krillitanes
Date   Comments

The Wire
Date   Comments

Ood
Date   Comments

The Beast
Date   Comments

The Isolus
Date   Comments